Da Vinci: His Life and His Legacy

Catherine McGrew Jaime

Other Non-Fiction Da Vinci Books by Catherine Jaime
Doing Da Vinci for Students
Exploring the Last Supper
In Art: Leonardo

Da Vinci Historical Fiction by Catherine
Leonardo the Florentine
Leonardo: Masterpieces in Milan
Leonardo: To Mantua and Beyond
Leonardo: A Return to Florence

Other Historical Fiction by Catherine:
York Proceeded On: The Lewis and Clark Expedition through the Eyes of Their Forgotten Member
The Gracie Jones Chronicles: Visiting the Vanderbilts
Failure in Philadelphia?
The Attack Trilogy

Creative Learning Connection
8006 Old Madison Pike, Ste 11-A
Madison, Alabama 35758
U.S.A.
www.CreativeLearningConnection.com

Table of Contents

"Study the science of art and the art of science."[1]

Introduction

Leonardo da Vinci lived at a time when people did not *specialize* in a particular area, like we tend to do today, and his life showed that trend clearly. May this little book *introduce* you to this incredible "Renaissance man"[2] – the artist, the scientist, the inventor, the architect, the fable teller, the cartographer, the anatomist, the mathematician.

* * * * * * * *

What makes this book different from others about Leonardo? Why take on a project like this, when so many others have already been written about him? Because, most books I read that were geared for kids had very little information, and those geared for adults generally had too much.

---

[1] Unless otherwise noted, quotes at the beginning of each chapter and the drawings scattered throughout the book are from Leonardo himself.

[2] According to the World Book Dictionary, a "Renaissance man" is "a man who is knowledgeable in an unusually wide variety of the arts and sciences" – and it describes Leonardo da Vinci as the "epitome of the 'Renaissance man'."

I have tried to make this book complete enough to give a good picture of who Leonardo was and what he accomplished, without overwhelming my readers. I have tried to make it interesting for those who may know nothing about Leonardo, and yet still interesting for those who already know quite a bit! I have also attempted to make it interesting enough for a wide range of ages – from kids of all ages through adults.

And I have attempted to place Leonardo in a framework of history and geography, so that we can more easily understand his accomplishments. The books I read about him often referred in passing to where he was and what was going on around him – without giving sufficient information to understand how those locations and events affected him. I have attempted to fill some of those gaps.

May we ponder the man, the works, and the accomplishments behind the stories of Leonardo da Vinci. May we be touched in some small way by this "Renaissance Man." And may we gain a better understanding of the times in which he lived.

* * * * * * * *

Leonardo's life can be divided into four basic periods:
1. The early years
2. The Milan years
3. The travel years
4. The final years

This book is divided into those same four sections. Within each section, I have included chapters that deal with the different topics that were an important part of Leonardo's life during those time periods.

"Many are they who have a taste and love for drawing..."

Note to Teachers/Parents

This book is intended for students and adults alike.

If this book leaves you or your students wanting more information – there is obviously no shortage out there. I have listed dozens of websites and books in the bibliography to get you started.[3] A couple of precautionary thoughts though:

1. Leonardo da Vinci was accused anonymously of inappropriate sexual behavior during his youth – the charges were dropped; there was no real proof, but some books and websites elaborate unnecessarily on the incident.

2. Leonardo studied human anatomy extensively, and countless numbers of his *drawings/sketches* show that interest – including many nudes. You may want to pick the books and websites your students look at

---

3 Caution is needed, as noted below, with even these books and websites.

accordingly.[4] None of his *paintings* have nudes – unless you count the occasional naked baby. In my book, I also took the liberty of "clothing" Leonardo's famous "Vitruvian Man"[5], because the principles he was illustrating with it are impressive, even if I don't fully appreciate the way Leonardo drew him.

3. Leonardo's parents were not married when he was born. (In fact they would both go on to marry other people.) I do mention that in the section about his family – without going into a lot of details. If you are reading this aloud to younger students, you may certainly skip those portions without losing critical information.

---

4 I found very few books or websites that could be shared with my students without a fair amount of creative editing first.
5 On page 105.

Leonardo in Western History

Dates	Related/Major World Events
Mid 1100's to c.1400	Gothic period in Art and Architecture *(So named by Renaissance humanists, referring to the "barbaric" art of the Middle Ages.)*
Mid 1300's	Renaissance begins in Italy.
1440	Printing Press is invented in Germany.
1452	Ottoman Sultan starts charging ships entering the Black Sea.
1453	Constantinople finally falls, bringing an end to the dying Byzantine Empire, *and strengthening the Ottoman Empire.*

Leonardo da Vinci came into this world at a time of great changes in the West.[6] Even architecture was changing, as domes were becoming more popular, due to the influence from "*the East.*"

---

6 "The West" refers to Europe, parts of Africa, and eventually North and South America and "the East" refers to the Orient and what we now call "the Middle East."

Map of Europe*

*This map shows the countries in Europe that were an important part of Leonardo's life and legacy, and three important cities: Anchiano, the city of his birth; Amboise, the city of his death; and Constantinople (which is now Istanbul).

Surprised to see Constantinople and Norway shown here? See the chapter "Leonardo's Bridge" for the answer to that mystery.

Map of Italy*

*Shows the places in Italy that Leonardo lived or visited for an extended period of time. (Italy was not a country yet – and many of the cities shown were independent city-states at the time.)

7

Early Years – Overview

Leonardo's early years were not particularly easy for him – he lived first with his mother, and then with his grandparents and uncle, and eventually with his father – changing locations each time. His formal education was very limited until he moved to Florence to apprentice with one of the greatest early artists of the Renaissance, Andrea del Verrocchio.

In addition to this great introduction to art, Leonardo was introduced to Renaissance architecture at this time. Domes were becoming popular in the West, first appearing in Florence, where Leonardo da Vinci spent so much of his early life. In fact, Donato Bramante, one of the greatest dome architects of their day, was working in Florence while Leonardo was there, and Leonardo interacted regularly with him.

In 1472, while still an apprentice, Leonardo was accepted into the local painters' guild. Leonardo continued as Verrocchio's apprentice for a while even after obtaining his status as a "true" painter. In 1477, at age 25, he finally opened his own studio, where he would have many of his own students.

.

Early Years
Leonardo's Family

"He would have been very proficient at his early lessons if he had not been so volatile and unstable; for he was always setting himself to learn many things only to abandon them almost immediately."
-- Vasari

Most biographies list Leonardo da Vinci's birthplace as the village of Vinci, though he was actually born in the nearby smaller village of Anchiano.[7] At that time Vinci and Anchiano were part of the city-state of Florence, not the country of Italy.[8]

Da Vinci's home in Anchiano

---

[7] Anchiano is harder to find on a map of Italy than Vinci!
[8] Italy would not become a united country until 1861.

Leonardo lived in Anchiano with his mother Caterina for the first few years of his life.[9] Very little is known about Leonardo's mother, who is presumed to have been a peasant, since his father did not marry her.[10]

It appears that Leonardo moved in with his father's family in Vinci when his mother married a few years later. Leonardo spent most of his pre-teen years with his uncle and grandparents at their country estate there. His father, Ser Piero, was a notary (a member of the legal profession) like his father and his father's father. Because Leonardo's parents were not married, the notary guild and the university[11] would be closed to him as he grew up.

Leonardo's formal education consisted of learning to read, write, and do basic math, all taught by the local parish priest. Throughout his life Leonardo referred to himself as "a man without an education." And yet, even though his formal education ended early, Leonardo was always studying and learning. He lived at a time when the newly invented printing press and cheaper paper were making books affordable. Over the years, though he was never a rich man, he owned many of his own books, and borrowed frequently from others. His quest for knowledge was never satiated.

---

[9] And she lived with him for the last few years of her life.

[10] At least one website I encountered suggested that Caterina may have been a slave from the Middle East.

[11] A guild was an organization that craftsmen and professionals had to belong to in the Middle Ages in order to do certain types of work.

Leonardo's father died at age 77 in 1504, with twelve children, ages six – 52.[12] He had been married four times. There was no will, and Leonardo's half-siblings made sure he didn't get any of the inheritance.

Leonardo's uncle died three years later, leaving everything to Leonardo. The siblings fought their uncle's will, the court ruled in their favor, and said that Leonardo could only USE the property until he died, when his siblings would get it! In addition to the financial burden each of these legal fights caused him, and the time the fighting took him away from his work; the larger pain to Leonardo was in being shut out, again and again, from his family.

Leonardo never married – he was seemingly more interested in his work than in establishing additional family relationships.

---

[12] Leonardo was the oldest by many years, since his father's first two wives bore him no children before they died.

Early Years
Leonardo, the Apprentice

"He is a poor disciple who does not excel his master."

Leonardo first moved to Florence with his father as a young teenager. At that time, Florence was the cultural center of Europe – effectively ruled by the Medici family, the richest family in Italy.

Leonardo apprenticed there to Andrea del Verrocchio, one of the most renowned artists of the day.[13] As an apprentice his first tasks were to make paintbrushes, to prepare canvases, and to learn how to mix paints. And like the other artists of his day, he then learned to make sculptures; to make patterns for tapestries and carpets; to paint banners for festivals; to make sets and costumes for pageants; and of course, to paint pictures. He also began to study architecture during this time in Florence.

Painting was not a prestigious occupation during the Middle Ages and the early Renaissance period. Paintings were

---

[13] In fact as a sculptor, Verrocchio had no peers during his lifetime. Leonardo apprenticed with Verrocchio with several other young men, for between six and ten years.

generally done only on commission for those who had money – such as government officials and churches. In fact, paintings were usually done by studios as "group efforts" with multiple artists working on several paintings at the same time. This is one of the reasons most paintings from that era are not signed.[14]

In 1472, Leonardo's teacher, Verrocchio, had done most of a painting of St. John baptizing Jesus for the *Baptism of Christ* painting (on the next page). Leonardo added the angel in the left corner. According to legends, the angel was so much better than what Verrocchio had painted, that Verrocchio said he would never paint again![15]

Leonardo's oldest drawing, the landscape shown at the beginning of the chapter was drawn at this time, also. It is possibly the oldest landscape drawing in the West. In the East, landscape drawings were already very popular, but western artists did only portraits and religious scenes prior to this time.

---

[14] Even when only one artist painted a picture, he didn't generally sign it, since there was no "pride" associated with the finished product. It was just an assignment to complete.

[15] It would have been a sound economic decision for the master – since he could leave the painting to his young apprentice, and concentrate on other money-making aspects of his business, such as sculpting.

Early Years
Leonardo, the Architect

Note to himself: "First write the treatise on the causes of the giving way of walls and then, separately, treat of the remedies."

Leonardo addressed the damages to a church structure, the St. Francesco al Monte. He also drew up plans for lifting yet another church, and putting a basement under it. He almost convinced the city planners to try his plan.

When the dome of another nearby church collapsed, Leonardo's interest in the strength and safety in buildings was piqued. One of Leonardo's architectural suggestions was to put a dance hall only on the bottom floor of a building, so that no one could be crushed beneath it if the weight and stress of the dancing became too much. He studied cracks in walls, and their causes. He studied the strength of building materials, domes, foundations, supports, beams, etc. He wrote of "the nature of the arch," and investigated what gave it its strength.

Leonardo's plans were varied – from churches to palaces to stables, to canals and locks. While his plans for most of those remained primarily at the plan level, some of his research and planning in locks and canals was actually carried out in his lifetime.

While most of Leonardo's architectural work was theoretical and not physical (or necessarily practical) he still contributed much to the field of architecture, with his studies, ideas, and his regular contact with the great architects of the day.[16] His notebooks contain such a wealth of information from this time frame that they almost fully cover the evolving High Renaissance styles of his day. We don't have any evidence that any of the buildings built during this time were fully designed by Leonardo da Vinci, but there are indications that he influenced many of them.

---

[16] Leonardo served almost in an "advisory" capacity to several of them.

Early Years
Leonardo, the Artist

"...art is a major path to knowledge."

Leonardo da Vinci was left-handed, but he actually painted on occasion with both hands.[17] Da Vinci often worked from clay models when he was in the studio painting or from the sketches in his notebooks. He did sketches with red chalk, black chalk, pen and ink, charcoal, and silverpoint.[18]

He considered art to be the "queen of all sciences." He took a small sketchbook with him everywhere. He frequently drew and studied the things around him. He advised his students: "When you go out for a walk, see to it that you watch and consider men's postures and actions as they talk, argue, laugh or scuffle together; their own actions and those of their

[17] Michelangelo was also capable of painting with both hands, and would often surprise visitors when he was painting his ceiling frescoes, by switching hands.
[18] Silverpoint was a popular way of drawing for Renaissance artists. They sketched first with charcoal, and then applied silverpoint (actually a *silver* pencil) over the charcoal. A small silverpoint drawing by Leonardo sold for $11 million in 2001.

supporters and onlookers, and make a note of these with a few strokes in your little book which you must always carry with you."

Like many other artists of the day, Leonardo worked on sculptures in addition to his paintings. Unfortunately, we have no evidence that any of his sculptures still exist.[19]

Leonardo learned to paint with the new Flemish technique, which used powdered colors mixed with oil instead of water. The large paintings generally began with:

1. Small sketches
2. Then actual size drawings
3. Then the transfer (holes through the drawing, almost like a "dot-to-dot")
4. Then the dark colored underpainting, which gave the pictures their depth
5. And finally, the bright colors.

Leonardo is credited with two new techniques which would change painting drastically, *chiaroscuro* – which deals with light and shade, and *sfumato* – which deals with blending colors / softening around the edges, almost a haze. Filippo Brunelleschi had recently developed rules for perspective in paintings, and Leonardo worked to incorporate perspective into his paintings as well.[20]

---

[19] And no evidence that he did a significant number of them either. He considered sculpting to be inferior to painting.
[20] Perspective gave paintings from the 15th century a much more realistic look than paintings from prior centuries.

From his own painting experiences, Leonardo developed numerous rules and concepts for painters that he cited in his notebooks. One of his "rules" was: "The mind of the painter should be like a mirror which always takes the color of the thing that it reflects, and which is filled by as many images as there are things placed before it."

Leonardo hoped to compile these notes into a book someday. He was personally unsuccessful, but eventually his notes were compiled into the book, *Treatise on Painting*, which was finally published in 1651.

The first painting believed to be done by Leonardo da Vinci that still exists is the *Portrait of Ginevera de Benici*; he painted it around 1474.[21] Unfortunately, he left most of his paintings unfinished over the years. He would give up on paintings at any point in the process when he got bored with them, or became interested in something else.

---

[21] Most of Leonardo's paintings were of young women and many of those were "Madonnas" (Mary and baby Jesus).

In his desire to be as accurate as possible, he was constantly moving into side interests – anatomy, botany, engineering, and more. Those other interests would often take him away from painting for quite a while. For all the fame attached to his painting, Leonardo completed many more sketches than he did paintings. Modern historians believe he only finished about twenty-five paintings in his lifetime, and less than twenty of those still exist today. (The only painting he actually signed was the *Mona Lisa*, so there is even dispute as to which paintings were actually done by Leonardo.)[22] His notebooks, on the other hand are filled with sketches – on almost every page of thousands of pages.

---

[22] Some of his drawings are signed, generally simply as "Leonardo."

Milan Years – Overview

Leonardo's last few years in Florence were in the employment of Duke Lorenzo de Medici. But, apparently he was ready to move on, looking for a new job. He wrote Ludovico Sforza, the Duke of Milan [23] an extensive letter requesting a job with him. The timing of the move was surprising, since, Leonardo had just received several big painting contracts in Florence. Because of that, some historians believe Leonardo was actually sent to Milan by the Duke of Florence, as a good-will gesture, rather than going of his own accord.

When Leonardo presented himself to the Duke, he took him a gift of a silver lyre that he had made in the shape of a horse's head.

This was an amazingly busy time in Leonardo's life. In addition to all he did for the Duke, Leonardo started his notebooks, worked on his music, painted *The Last Supper*, and designed an equestrian monument. Leonardo may have also studied in Pavia for a number of months during this time period, examining both mathematics and science closely there.

In 1485 and 1486 plagues devastated Milan, killing thousands. In the aftermath, Leonardo collaborated with Duke Ludovico to rebuild the city. His plans included ideas for a system of water flowing through the city to improve sanitation.[24] He also drew plans for two sets of streets, one

---

[23] Milan was also a fairly powerful city-state in northern Italy.
[24] Actually a good idea, but never put into effect.

for "vehicles" and one for pedestrians. Locks were built in Milan in 1497 according to his plans.

PROJET DE VILLE SUR DEUX NIVEAUX, vers 1488. Dessin à la plume   DRAFT OF A TOWN ON TWO LEVELS, circa 1488. Pen and ink drawing

When Milan fell to French troops, Duke Ludovico fled, and Leonardo da Vinci and his new friend, the mathematician Luca Pacioli, left together, and traveled together to Vaprio and to Mantua.

Milan Years
Leonardo and the Duke

"If you want to build an armada for the sea, employ these ships to ram in the enemy's ships...."

When Leonardo wrote Ludovico Sforza, the Duke of Milan [25], his extensive letter, it was as if what Leonardo *wanted* to do was more important in his own mind than what he had already done. In spite of all Leonardo's abilities, the Duke most likely hired him to build a statue to the Duke's father. (But more on that later.) The text of Leonardo's letter, his "resume," to the Duke follows:

To My Lord the Duke of Milan,
Florence, 1482

Most Illustrious Lord,

Having until now sufficiently considered the specimens of all those who proclaim themselves skilled contrivers of

---

[25] Milan was also a fairly powerful "city-state" in northern Italy, ruled by a Duke.

instruments of war, and that the invention and operation of the said instruments are nothing different to those in common use:

I shall endeavor, without prejudice to any one else, to explain myself to your Excellency showing your Lordship my secrets, and then offering them to your best pleasure and approbation to work with effect at opportune moments as well as all those things which in part, shall be briefly noted below:

1. I have a sort of extremely light and strong bridges, adapted to be most easily carried, and with them you may pursue, and at any time flee from the enemy; and others, secure and indestructible by fire and battle, easy and convenient to lift and place. Also methods to burn and destroy those of the enemy.

2. I know how, when a place is besieged, to take the water out of the trenches, and make endless variety of bridges, and covered ways and ladders, and other machines pertaining to such expeditions.

3. Item, If by reason of the height of the banks, or the strength of the place and its position, it is impossible, when besieging a place, to avail oneself of the plan of bombardment, I have methods for destroying every rock or other fortress, even if it were founded on a rock, etc.

4. Again, I have kinds of mortars; most convenient and easy to carry; and with these can fling small stones almost resembling a storm; and with the smoke of these causing great terror to the enemy, to his great detriment and confusion.

5. And when the fight should be at sea I have kinds of many machines most efficient for offence and defense; and vessels which will resist the attack of the largest guns and powder and fumes.

6. Item, I have means by secret and tortuous mines and ways, made without noise to reach a designated spot, even if it were need to pass under a trench or a river.

7. I will make covered chariots, safe and unattackable which, entering among the enemy with their artillery, there is no body of men so great but they would break them. And behind these, infantry could follow quite unhurt and without any hindrance.

8. In case of need I will make big guns, mortars and light ordinance of fine and useful forms, out of the common type.

9. Where the operation of bombardment should fail, I would contrive catapults...and other machines of marvelous efficacy and not in common use. And in short, according to the variety of cases, I can contrive various and endless means of offence and defense...

10. In time of peace I believe I can carry out sculpture in marble, bronze, or clay, and also in painting whatever may be done, and as well as any other, be he whom he may.

Again the bronze horse may be taken in hand, which is to be to the immortal glory and eternal honour of the prince your father of happy memory, and of the illustrious house of Sforza.

And if any one of the above-named things seem to any one to be impossible or not feasible, I am most ready to make the experiment in your park, or in whatever place may please your Excellency – to whom I commend myself with the utmost humility.

Leonardo da Vinci

Since war was always a concern for the Duke, Leonardo emphasized his ideas for offensive and defensive war machines more than his artistic abilities.[26] The Duke didn't actually answer Leonardo's letter, but Leonardo moved to Milan the next year, when he was about thirty-years-old, and there received the title of "painter and engineer of the duke."

---

[26] Even though, throughout his life, Leonardo professed a hatred of war, and the casualties it causes.

Leonardo's first job in Milan was to paint a church altarpiece[27] – which he painted completely contrary to the contract he had signed with the monks. He showed Mary with Jesus and his cousin John as babies. But, the altarpiece was very beautiful and very popular. In all, Leonardo would only complete about six paintings during his lengthy stay in Milan, though his students undoubtedly completed others.

The Duke kept Leonardo busy after that, working on a heating system; painting portraits; making cannons and other weapons; building canals; and planning and designing pageants and entertainments for special occasions.

Leonardo also got very serious about his science studies during his years in Milan, and began recording copious notes in his notebooks.

---

[27] Altarpieces were the decorative art (usually Bible scenes) behind the altar in churches – and were often quite fancy in those days.

Milan Years
Leonardo, the Musician

"These two flutes do not change their tone by leaps as most wind instruments do, but in the manner of the human voice."

Like so much else he did, music seemed almost a passing interest for Leonardo da Vinci. But he was reputed to be quite an accomplished musician. Leonardo was fond of singing, and liked to accompany himself with a lute or a lyre.[28] He was well-known during his life for his "impromptu" performances for his friends, and very little of his music was recorded in his notebooks. Leonardo was fascinated by drums, bells, and organ pipes. When he worked on designs for churches, acoustics were a special concern.

---

[28] Also referred to as a "lira" or "lira de braccio."

Leonardo spent much of his "inventing" time trying to perfect existing musical instruments, as well as trying to develop new ones. He combined his anatomy studies with his musical understanding to develop instruments that worked properly with the limitations of human finger movement and the voice box.

There are some legends circulating that Leonardo invented the violin, which is quite similar to the lyre he liked to play. It's unlikely that he invented it,[29] though he may have contributed in a limited way to its design. He also had designs for an instrument that resembled an early piano.

---

[29] Since most historians date the violin's history back to several decades *after* his death.

Milan Years Leonardo, the Mathematician

One of Leonardo's patrons complained: "He is so much distracted from painting by his mathematical experiments as to become intolerant of the brush."

In 1482, Euclid's geometry book *Elements* became available in printed form in Latin.[30] After almost 1,800 years of neglect, interest in geometry was slowly being revitalized.[31] Leonardo taught himself Latin as an adult, so that he could better read classics such as this.

Leonardo met Luca Pacioli, a traveling monk, when they were both working in Milan for the Duke. When Pacioli wrote his own study of mathematics, *De divina proportione* ("*On Divine Proportion*"), he asked Leonardo to provide sixty illustrations for it, as well as some mathematical assistance.

---

[30] Euclid had written *Elements* in Greek almost 1800 years earlier.
[31] Modern geometry "officially" began over one hundred years after Leonardo, in the early 1600's, but interest in the subject was slowly being rekindled in his day.

Later when Leonardo began designing his famous horse statue (more about that later!), Pacioli helped him with the mathematical problems he faced.

In Leonardo's mind, mathematics went hand in hand with both art and science, and could not really be separated totally from either of them. But for a time, Leonardo was more focused on his mathematical studies than he was on his painting.

Milan Years
Leonardo, the Scientist

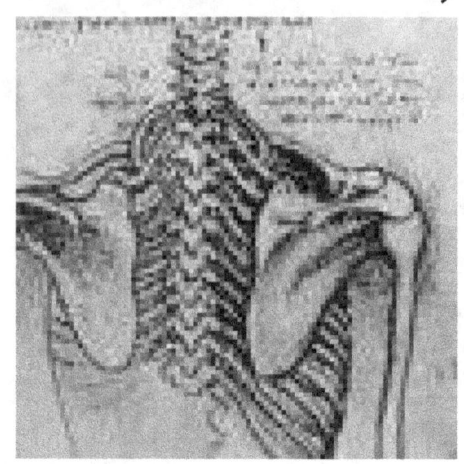

"From science is born creative action, which is of much more value."

Leonardo da Vinci is considered by many to be the first modern scientist. In his mind and actions, art and science were intimately connected. He used art to improve his science studies, and science to improve his art. He conducted experiments to confirm the observations he made.

He:
- Observed
- Questioned
- Made hypotheses
- Experimented
- Measured:
  - Humidity
  - Altitude
  - Distance traveled
  - Speed of wind
  - Motion of water
  - Intensity of Light

Scientific Topics Leonardo studied included:

- Anatomy
  > As he learned more about the human body, Leonardo wrote: *"A wonderful instrument, the invention of the supreme master."*

- Astronomy
  > *"I say that as the moon has no light in itself and yet is luminous, it is inevitable but that its light is caused by some other body."*

- Botany
  > *"A leaf always turns its upper side towards the sky so that it may better receive, on all its surface, the dew which drops gently from the atmosphere."*

- Creation vs. Evolution[32]
  > *"Why do we find the bones of great fishes and oysters and corals and various other shells and sea-snails on the high summits of mountains by the sea, just as we find them in low seas?"*

- Geology
  > *"Mountains are made by the currents of rivers. Mountains are destroyed by the currents of rivers."*

- Mechanics
  > *"Mechanics are the paradise of mathematical science, because here we come to the fruit of mathematics."*

---

[32] Leonardo didn't believe in Creation, or even "the great flood," but he constantly struggled to get his observations to match his beliefs.

- Optics

    "When both eyes direct the pyramid of sight to an object, that object becomes clearly seen and comprehended by the eyes."

- Zoology

    "The smallest feline is a masterpiece."

- and much more...

Leonardo's understanding of optics led him to improvements in shadows and perspective in painting, and his knowledge of geology and geography improved the quality of the landscapes he drew and painted. And his knowledge of anatomy improved the realism in the human figures he drew and painted.

Milan Years
Leonardo's Notebooks

"He labored much more by his word than in fact or deed."[33]
--Vasari

Leonardo made a practice of always carrying a small notebook with him and then copying his notes, sketches, etc. onto larger sheets each evening.

Leonardo's notebooks were unique for many reasons: In his notebooks, the words typically accompanied the pictures, instead of vice versa. He started his notes on the "back page." He wrote backwards, possibly because he was left-handed and could avoid smearing his ink if he wrote from right to left across the page; or possibly to keep his work "secret," or at least make it harder to read.[34] Leonardo used no punctuation

---

[33] In the early biography of Leonardo da Vinci by Giorgio Vasari.

[34] I personally lean towards the first reason. Writing backwards was probably more efficient for his left handed style, and that's what was important to Leonardo! He was capable of writing "correctly" – he just didn't do it often.

in his notebooks; sometimes he wrote in code and/or shorthand; and he often ran words together. He also wrote some of his notes in Italian and some in Latin after he started learning that language. Needless to say, deciphering his notebooks has been an arduous task!

Leonardo's notebooks were generally unorganized, usually consisting of loose pages, that he only occasionally bound himself. They contained notes about four major categories: anatomy, architecture, mechanics, and painting. His notebooks also included:

- o Astronomy
- o Botany
- o Drafts of letters
- o Drawings
- o Geology
- o Geography
- o Geometry
- o Invention plans
- o Lists of books
- o Maps he had drawn
- o Menus from what he had eaten recently
- o Nature observations
- o Notes from borrowed books
- o Water
- o Weapons

Leonardo's Map of Tuscany

A number of comprehensive studies were printed in Leonardo's lifetime on architecture and painting. Leonardo had big plans to publish his own notes as early as 1498, and several times after that, as a sort of "encyclopedia" of many subjects, but unfortunately he died before he ever finished that project. He willed his notebooks to one of his students who didn't get them published either. When his student died, the notebooks were forgotten, and over the years they were divided up, sold, stored, and some were even destroyed. For almost three centuries the notebooks were basically lost and/or forgotten, keeping Leonardo da Vinci from being considered the "first" in many scientific endeavors.

More than 7,000 pages from Leonardo's notebooks have been recovered.[35] No other artist or scientist, before or since, has left the kind of "paper trail" that Leonardo da Vinci left – his notebooks were like his journal, sketchbook, scrapbook, and log book, all rolled into one.

Pages from notebooks have been found in obscure places throughout Europe, some even recently, and now the collections mostly reside in major museums in England, Spain, Italy, and France, though some are also in private hands.[36]

His notebook pages have been gathered into at least ten different "major" collections, such as the Codex Arundel, Codex Atlanticus, Codex Trivulianus, and at least forty "minor" ones. The pages in these collections range in size from 3" x 4" to 8.5" x 12"[37] and each set has anywhere from one page to 238 pages. The notebooks are probably dated between 1473 and 1516, though the exact dates of many of them are not known. Most of the collections have been bound in "modern times"; bound in leather, parchment, or cardboard.

---

[35] It is believed that there were at least 14,000 pages originally.
[36] Bill Gates bought one of the collections in 1995.
[37] Between 7x9 centimeters, and 22x29 centimeters.

Milan Years
Leonardo, the Engineer and Inventor

"The perseverance to pursue it and to invent such things...is found in few people."

Many of Leonardo's "inventions" never went beyond the planning stage, often because he was "ahead of his time." Centuries later, many of his ideas were actually built: the helicopter, the tank, the machine gun, the parachute, the bicycle, the wheelbarrow – all existed in Leonardo's mind and notebooks long before they came to be. Our family has a book on the history of tanks. Leonardo's "tank," shown above, is shown first in that historical reference.

One hundred years before Galileo used a telescope to look at the stars, Leonardo was considering the possibility of "making glasses with which...to view the moon at an enlarged size."

Leonardo wanted to save people time with many of his inventions – and he used all of the common "helpers" of his day – screws, pulleys, fly wheels, and springs. Many of these he used in new and unusual ways, and often in plans that went beyond the materials available in his day. A museum near his birthplace has 3-D models of fifty-five of Leonardo's "inventions" and machines. His plans were varied, including a wide variety of ideas:

- Aerial Screw
- Automatic Roasting Spit
- Bicycle
- Clock
- Diving Bell
- Diving Suit
- Double Crane
- Drilling Machine
- Eye Glasses
- Fan
- Flying Ship
- Hang Glider
- Helicopter
- Horseless Wagon
- Lens Grinding Machine (for mirrors)
- Locks for Canals
- Machine Gun
- Mechanical Drum
- Monkey Wrench
- Naval Cannon
- Oil Lamp that gave out brighter light
- Paddle Boat
- Parachute
- Pontoon Bridges
- Projector
- Pulleys

- Revolving Bridge
- Revolving Crane
- Screw-thread Cutter
- Self-propelled Car
- Spinning Wheel improvements
- Submarine
- Tank
- Telescope
- Temporary Bridges
- Water Pump
- Water Wheel
- Wheel Barrow
      to name "a few"...

Leonardo worked with water (an especially important commodity in his day) – designing water towers, and canals and locks. We can go today to see locks and canals that Leonardo sketched out and planned centuries ago, and even in our own time and area, we can enjoy the benefit of these "far-fetched" ideas of a forward-looking Leonardo da Vinci.

Milan Years
Leonardo's Horse

"Of the horse, I shall say nothing because I know the times."

Duke Galeazzo Sforza had inherited the dukedom of Milan upon his father's death. The idea of a statue to honor his father, the man responsible for bringing Milan its independence, had gnawed at him for some time. After Galeazzo's murder, power passed to Galeazzo's young son, and then quickly to Galeazzo's brother, Ludovico. Ludovico liked the idea of a monument as well – a horse with a rider on its back representing their father, the soldier-hero.

In fact, Ludovico may have hired Leonardo specifically thinking of this project. Leonardo had mentioned the horse project almost in passing at the end of his letter to the duke. He had helped his master, Verrocchio, in his research for an equestrian statue during his days as an apprentice in Florence.[38]

---

[38] Verrocchio in Venice in 1488, and Donatello in Padua in 1453, had both completed equestrian monuments to military heroes, both of which Leonardo would also have been familiar with.

Original plans called for the statue to be life-size, with the horse in a rearing position. It was an interesting project for Leonardo to even contemplate – considering his attitude toward sculpting.[39]

While working on *The Last Supper*, Leonardo would also work on his horse sculpture. As with his other projects, Leonardo could not be rushed. He spent years studying horses, even dissecting a few, to make sure he understood how their muscles worked together. He also spent years on the design for the monument, visiting many other similar statues in the area. His had to be better than all the others! Of course, by 1485, three years after hiring Leonardo, the Duke was getting impatient to have his monument completed, and by 1489 he was actually looking for another artist to take over the project.

It didn't help that over time, the Duke also changed his mind about what he wanted: He decided his statue should be four times life-size, which would make it the largest monument of its kind in that day.

---

[39] Leonardo considered sculpting to be much inferior to painting!

The horse was now to be twenty-four feet tall. To accommodate the larger size, Leonardo had to change the positioning of the horse from rearing to standing. He also worked hard to develop a new system for casting the statue, so it could be cast in one piece.[40] Leonardo did not want to use the current system of "lost wax" casting, which caused a number of problems, including that the mold was never reusable in this method.[41] He invented a new way to use a double mold to make the cast.[42] And he planned to cast the horse upside down, to resolve some of the problems with the weight in a statue of this size.

By 1493, just in time for the wedding of Bianca Sforza, daughter of the Duke of Milan, and Emperor Maximilian, Leonardo unveiled a twenty-four-feet tall clay model of the horse. It was beautiful, and people came from miles away to

---

[40] Something that had never been done for a statue of this size.

[41] In the "lost-wax" method, a model was made out of wax, the mold would be made over the wax – and then the wax was melted out and replaced with bronze.

[42] In 1699 someone would finally try Leonardo's double mold method. It worked, and a statue of King Louis XIV was made with it – which lasted almost100 years until it was destroyed during the French Revolution.

gaze at it. In 1494 he finally began preparing the molds for the actual statue.

The amount of metal needed to cast was tremendous, approximately eighty tons, and Leonardo worked to collect it while he "perfected" his design and technique. Unfortunately, Milan was attacked by France in 1499 and had to use the dedicated metal for cannon balls.

Leonardo was quoted as saying at that time, "Of the horse I shall say nothing because I know the times."

Milan still lost the battle with the French, the Duke fled, and so did Leonardo. The French archers used his huge clay horse for target practice, and it eventually crumbled into nothing.

In 1508 Leonardo would be invited to make a statue for the Italian general, Trivulzio, who had led the French troops against Milan. Leonardo actually worked on plans for it, but that statue was never completed either.

Leonardo would lament the unfinished horse for the rest of his life.

* * * * *

In 1966, 467 years after the French invasion halted the equine project, sketches of Leonardo da Vinci's horse were rediscovered in Spain.

In 1977 *National Geographic* ran a very short piece about "The Horse That Never Was." Charles Dent, a United Airlines pilot, read the article, and became very interested in finally building Leonardo's horse as a gift to Italy.

Over the next seventeen years, Charles Dent raised money, had a special dome built to work in, studied horses, came up with an initial design and got the first life size model of the horse completed[43]...

In 1994, he died, before the work had been completed. His foundation, *Leonardo da Vinci's Horse, Inc.*, continued, and in 1996 the first attempt at an enlarged model failed. Something would have to be done differently with the eight foot model, and a new sculptor, Nina Akamu, was hired to finish work on *The Horse*. In 1998, Akamu's new eight foot model was completed, followed quickly by a twenty-four-foot clay model. Work was progressing.

On September 10, 1999, exactly five hundred years after the soldiers had destroyed Leonardo's clay model, Charles Dent and Leonardo da Vinci's dream horse was unveiled in Milan, Italy.[44] Nina Akamu had completed their project. *The Horse* stands proudly there on a marble pedestal.[45]

Seeing Da Vinci's Horse was one of the highlights of a visit to Milan, Italy!

---

[43] He decided to do just a horse, without a rider.
[44] Total costs for the project exceeded $4 million.
[45] Jean Fritz wrote a great children's book, *Leonardo's Horse*, about both Leonardo's work on the horse, and Dent's project almost 500 years later.

In October 1999 one more casting was made from the mold, this time for *The American Horse*, which now stands proudly at the Frederik Meijer Gardens in Grand Rapids, Michigan. This horse stands on the ground, rather than on a pedestal, so that visitors can walk right up to it.

In the year 2,000, a fifteen inch scale model of Leonardo's horse was given to the people of Milan to go with *Leonardo's Horse*. It is known as "the Horse for the Blind" – a miniature that can be "seen" by the blind, by touching it. In November 2001, an eight-foot replica of *Leonardo's Horse* was donated to Leonardo's home town.

And so, Leonardo's "Horse That Never Was" finally *is*, in multiple places!

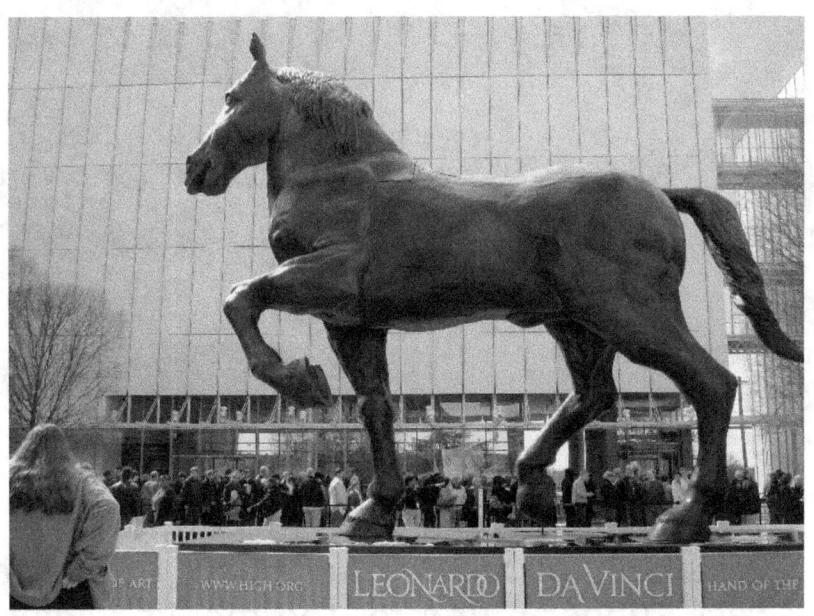

*A copy of Da Vinci's Horse was even in
Atlanta, Georgia for a time.*

Milan Years
The Last Supper

"When you wish to represent a man speaking to a number of people, consider the matter of which he has to treat and adapt his action to the subject. Thus if he speaks persuasively, let his action be appropriate to it..."

46

In 1495, three years after Columbus discovered the New World, while working for the Duke of Milan, Leonardo da Vinci started his *Last Supper* mural for the monks' dining room at the Santa Maria delle Grazie in Milan.[47]

---

46 This engraving was based on Leonardo's mural of the Last Supper.
[47] Donato Bramante was working on the dome there at the same time.

The Last Supper was a popular theme for frescos before and since his day, but Leonardo chose to do it in a unique manner – painting the disciples in groups of three at the table, each reacting to Christ's statement, "One of you will betray me." Additionally, he chose to depict "modern day" clothes, foods, and dishes for the picture, instead of those from the New Testament era, so that the monks of the Santa Maria delle Grazie monastery could relate better to it.

Even before he could start painting, Leonardo had to do countless sketches in preparation. He wanted each detail to be perfect. He agonized the longest over the faces for Christ and for Judas. One story is that he had to go to the worst part of Milan to find a face horrible enough to use for his model of Judas.

Another legend is that he inadvertently used the same person as his model for both Christ and Judas, a man who had become hardened in the years between the two portions of the picture. Christ and Judas were the last two faces he did so not much time separated the painting of the two of them, and so that story is unlikely. And yet a third legend is that the head monk complained to Leonardo that he was taking too long to finish the painting, and Leonardo offered to use HIS face for the model for Judas...bringing an end to that complaint.

Unfortunately, *The Last Supper* was yet another of Leonardo's experiments, since he didn't like the current way of painting frescos. Fresco painting techniques required an artist to apply wet plaster to a section of a wall, and then paint that section quickly with water-based paints. This method effectively bonded the paint to the plaster – which is why even after centuries, frescoes done this way have vibrant colors.

Leonardo wanted to paint slowly, and to be able to make changes as he went along. He developed a new paint solution of varnish and oil which he could use on a dry wall and change along the way. Because Leonardo was a perfectionist, and was distracted by other projects, he spent many years working on the mural.[48] Sadly, Leonardo had not perfected his new technique, and even in his lifetime the paint of his incredible *Last Supper* mural began to flake off the wall.

---

[48] Which would end up being 30 feet across by 14 feet high.

The Last Supper has suffered greatly since then as well. The monks wanted to protect it at one point, and hung a curtain over it, opening it only for special visitors. Unfortunately, the curtain scratched the painting as it went back and forth. In addition, it trapped moisture between the curtain and the wall, causing more damage.

In 1652, monks cut a door in the wall where *The Last Supper* is painted, cutting out the feet of Christ in the process. At another point, in 1796, French soldiers under Napoleon staying in the monastery defaced the painting by throwing things at it.[49]

During World War II, the wall was reinforced, and sand bags were placed behind the wall with the painting. A bomb hit the monastery only a few feet away from the wall, fortunately causing no more damage to the painting.

Over the centuries, starting in the 18th century, and then again in the 19th century, many artists have attempted to "restore" *The Last Supper*, often making the situation worse in the process. A major restoration was begun in 1977. An artist, Dr. Pinin Brambilla Barcilon, worked on the mural with a small microscope, removing centuries of dirt and grime, and the extra paint that had been applied since Leonardo's day. Twenty-two years later, she finally finished the project, which unfortunately met with mixed reviews from art critics around the world. Some thought she had gone too far with the removal of the paint, though others thought she had done an incredible job.

---

[49] Napoleon had actually ordered them not to mess up the painting, but they disobeyed.

The Last Supper is a masterpiece, and ranks with Leonardo's *Mona Lisa* for the fame associated with it. Even in Leonardo's lifetime, it was appreciated. When the French King, Louis XII, saw the painting, he was so impressed by it – he wanted to take it back to France – wall and all! Obviously not a practical idea, so the painting stayed where it was. All over the world, copies of it hang on home and church walls alike.

Milan Years
Leonardo's Robot

"I wish to work miracles"[50]

It is thought by some that Leonardo's focus on the measurements and mechanics of the human body came from his desire to build a human-type robot. The Institute and Museum of the History of Science in Florence, Italy recently did a computer analysis of some of Leonardo's drawings, proving that he had indeed made plans for a robot. His robot design included a jaw that opened and closed, a head that moved back and forth, and arms that could wave. His robot was to be dressed as a medieval knight.

Of course, Leonardo didn't call his mechanical man a "robot" – that word wouldn't come into usage until 1921, when humanoid robots would appear in a science fiction play, and decades more would pass before one would actually be built.

The plans for a humanoid robot in Leonardo's notebooks are dated as early as 1495, making it very probably the first humanoid robot ever designed. There's no proof that Leonardo ever built the robot, though some people argue that he did – but one was built recently, based on his plans.

---

[50] A comment Leonardo made about his anatomy work.

Travel Years — Overview

When Duke Ludovico lost Milan to the French in 1499, Leonardo left the city searching for new employment. He would spend many of the next six years wandering across Italy, during which time he did very little artistic work, but a significant amount of scientific work. He traveled first to Vaprio and Mantua, then on to Venice, and eventually he returned to Florence for a brief stay.

In 1502, he took one of his most unusual assignments, working for Cesare Borgia, military dictator for almost a year, traveling throughout the region of Romagna during much of that time. During that same year, he submitted plans to the Ottoman Sultan for a bridge the Sultan wanted to build over the mouth of the Black Sea.

When Leonardo tired of that work, he took a commission in Florence, and returned there, as a "local hero." During the next few years he traveled between Florence and Milan several times, often in an attempt to settle family issues caused by the lack of a will at his father's death, or a contested will after his uncle's death. Leonardo's most significant artwork during this time was his famous *Mona Lisa* painting.

Travel Years
Leonardo,
the Military Advisor

"If the fortress can be attacked only from a single side, make that side in the form of a massive acute angle of 25 – 30 feet, with its lateral defenses..."

From 1499 – 1502, Cesare Borgia, son of Pope Alexander VI and military dictator, was ruthless in his attempt to gain power over Romagna, a central portion of Italy.[51] He was encouraged in his efforts by the Pope. Leonardo worked for Borgia as "senior military architect and general engineer" during much of that time, and met Niccolo Machiavelli, who was also working for Borgia. (Many years later Machiavelli would write his most famous book, *The Prince*, significantly based on the unscrupulous means by which Borgia conquered and ruled.)

---

[51] Italy was not a unified country at the time – it was mostly comprised of independent city-states who were constantly fighting each other for power, as well as fighting France, Spain, Germany, and the Ottoman Empire.

As advisor to Borgia, Leonardo traveled throughout central Italy – Imola, Cesena, Rimini, Urbino, and Pesaro. He gave recommendations for military improvements, as well as accurately mapping the region.

Map of Imola created by da Vinci for Cesare Borgia.

Later he was in Piombino to improve the fortifications of the town Borgia had just taken from Jacopo Appiani.

Later, back in Florence, Leonardo worked with Machiavelli for over a year trying to divert the Arno River with canals, for military and transportation purposes. It would have involved tunneling through the Serravalle Mountain Pass.[52]

After the downfall of Borgia, Leonardo went back to Piombino briefly. Here Machiavelli was attempting a diplomatic mission, when Leonardo came to advise the new/old leader, Appiani, on the city's fortifications. Leonardo's recommendations included a tunnel or moat, trenches, and the leveling of some hills outside the fortifications. He also planned for some improvements to the towers, including the placement of cannon there (He was the first military architect to suggest that).

For a man who despised war, Leonardo spent much time advising those who practiced it![53]

---

[52] The tunneling and canals were not done until modern times, and Leonardo's exact route was used.

[53] Possibly out of a false sense of loyalty, but more likely for the money – since he frequently needed to worry about who his next patron would be.

Travel Years
Leonardo's Bridge

"I have plans for bridges..."

Top View

Side View

While Leonardo da Vinci was serving Borgia, he was offered another unique assignment. This time it was Sultan Bajazet II, ruler of the Ottoman Empire, who considered hiring Leonardo.

The Sultan had sent ambassadors to the region of Italy to find engineers to design a bridge over the Golden Horn, an inlet of the Bosphorus, at the mouth of the Black Sea. Leonardo drew up plans for the Sultan's bridge, shown above. The Sultan and his advisors thought Leonardo's bridge, a giant arch shape, [54] was too radical, and that it would not be strong enough in the middle. [55] The Sultan requested that Michelangelo submit an alternate set of plans, but he was busy in Rome, and declined the offer. The Sultan never got his bridge built – and bridges were not built across the Golden Horn until 1836 and 1845.

---

[54] You have to look closely at the bottom portion of the drawing to see the arch shape.
[55] Had it been built, it would have been the longest bridge of its day.

Leonardo's bridge was forgotten about for many centuries until a Norwegian artist saw the plans at a Leonardo da Vinci exhibit in 1996, and "fell in love" with Leonardo's idea. The Norwegian artist, Vebjorn Sand, convinced the Norwegian Highway Department to build a scaled down version of the bridge. In 2002, Norwegian Queen Sonja unveiled the beautiful arch bridge, designed five hundred years earlier by Leonardo da Vinci.

Throughout his long and varied career,
da Vinci made other plans for bridges as well.

Travel Years
Battle of Anghiari
Painting

Leonardo on how to represent a battle: *"First you must represent the smoke of artillery mingling in the air with the dust and tossed up by the movement of horses and the combatants. And this mixture you must express thus..."*

In 1503, city officials in Florence wanted frescos painted on the walls of their new City Hall, and invited the now famous Leonardo and Michelangelo to paint them. It became a contest of sorts between the two painters, who did not get along particularly well.[56] Leonardo chose to paint the *Battle of Anghiari* on his wall, and Michelangelo went to work on the *Battle of Cascina*.[57] (These wall frescoes were to be more than twice as large as *The Last Supper* mural, which Leonardo had already completed.)[58]

---

[56] Among other things, Michelangelo, the "young upstart," had mocked Leonardo for his failed equestrian monument.
[57] Both were important victories against Pisa in Florence's past.
[58] 23 x 56 feet

Both Michelangelo and Leonardo prepared their initial "cartoons"[59] fairly quickly – to show how they intended to paint their walls. Leonardo especially wanted to insure that he had the angry faces of battle correct, the horses in the right positions, etc. He would not even begin painting the wall for almost two years.

Unfortunately, Leonardo chose another experimental technique, since he was still not happy with the available fresco techniques. This time the problem was that the paint would not dry. To correct the situation, Leonardo had assistants raise pots of hot oil on ropes up and down next to the wall. Unfortunately, the paint did not dry in the process – it ran instead, completely obliterating the painting Leonardo had done. Rather than go back and fix his mess, Leonardo just walked away from the job. Michelangelo never finished his wall either, being called off to Rome before he completed it. All that remains of the paintings are the sketches in Leonardo's notebook and copies of the walls painted by contemporary artists.

---

[59] Their large sketches showing the way the compositions would be painted.

*Peter Paul Reuben's copy of a copy
of a section of Leonardo's mural.*

The city officials of Florence would later complain that Leonardo had taken money for payment for a project he didn't finish. Eventually Leonardo would offer to pay the money back, and the officials would graciously decline.

Travel Years
Leonardo and Flight

"Feathers shall raise men even as they do birds..."

Leonardo da Vinci was fascinated by flight, and the idea of humans flying. He spent much time observing birds in flight, and dreaming of ways to fly. He analyzed how they flew, and the effects of wind and air resistance on their wings. Many of his notebook pages dealing with flight are dated 1505. In 1508 one of his assistants was injured, trying out one of Leonardo's flying contraptions.

In the East, kites had been in existence long before Leonardo's day, and sometimes he is mistakenly credited for "inventing" them in the West. There is no proof of this, but rather it results from confusion caused by a story from his early childhood: "...among the reflections of my infancy, it seemed to me that, as I was in my cradle, a kite came to me...and struck me several times with its tail..." This kite, in his story, was a bird, in the hawk family!

Leonardo drew designs for a helicopter and a parachute. And even though he would not live to see men fly, his ideas and designs are often listed first in studies of "the history of flight." Four hundred years after Leonardo da Vinci drew flying contraptions in the pages of his notebooks, the Wright brothers realized his dream of flying.

Travel Years
Mona Lisa

60

"Let your shadings melt away like smoke, like the sounds of soft music."

After attending eight classes and two workshops about Leonardo da Vinci, my 10-year-old has decided to write her own book on Leonardo. Her book currently begins: "Leonardo was a famous artist. Most of the reason he was so famous is because of the Mona Lisa, his most beloved of all..."

It is an intriguing picture – the smile, the veil, the hands that hold nothing, the unusual landscape in the background, the position of the sitter...In fact, the *Mona Lisa* is perhaps the single most famous painting in the world, but it is a surprisingly small painting, measuring only 21" X 30" (Or 53 cm X 77 cm). Its fame and mystery far exceed its size.

---

[60] These hands are considered by some to be from Leonardo's sketches for the *Mona Lisa*. For some reason, there are no other sketches in Leonardo's notebooks that go with the *Mona Lisa*. And yet, there seems to be no question as to its authenticity as "a da Vinci." One possibility is that the sketches he made for it are in the 7,000 or so pages missing from his notebooks!

The first debate about this intriguing work is over the identity of the woman in the painting.[61] Most (but not all) historians[62] agree that she was Lisa, the wife of Franceso del Giocondo,[63] from whence comes our English name for the picture. [64] Her smile has also intrigued people for a long time; Leonardo may have employed musicians to keep her happy during her sitting time.

The next mystery is why Leonardo never gave up the painting during his lifetime. He had been commissioned to paint it while still living in Italy, and he worked on it for at least four years there,[65] but it was one of the three paintings he took with him when he moved to France. [66] He apparently never considered it completed, or at least that's what he kept telling the man who had contracted with him for the picture! It is possible that he continued to work on it off and on during all those years. That certainly would have fit with his personality and work style.

King Francis I was very impressed with the painting, and offered to buy it from Leonardo. Leonardo was reluctant to

---

[61] Some art critics have gone so far as to say that the painting is really a self-portrait of Leonardo. I've even seen computerized images trying to prove that point. I don't believe a word of it!

[62] Starting with Leonardo's first biographer, Giorgio Vasari, in 1547, who dedicated ten pages of his *Great Lives of Artists* book to Leonardo da Vinci (Michelangelo received seventy-five pages).

[63] Lisa would have been an "upper middle class" Florentine lady, wife and mother.

[64] The Italians call her *La Gioconda* and the French call her *La Joconde*.

[65] Leonardo spent as much time on this one small painting as Michelangelo had spent on an entire ceiling fresco.

[66] The other two pictures were *St John the Baptist* and the *Virgin and Child with Saint Anne*.

part with it, but also wanted to please his new patron.[67] They struck an interesting deal: The king paid for the painting, but Leonardo kept it in his new home in France, and when Leonardo died, the king took possession of it. Which is why the most famous painting in the world was painted by an Italian, but hangs in a French museum.[68]

Of course, it didn't begin its "career" as the most famous painting in the world, it had to work its way up to that position. Even in Leonardo's lifetime it was a popular painting, Raphael had seen it while Leonardo was still working on it, and was impressed by it. Other painters were soon copying it. Soon after Leonardo's death, the biographer Vasari was already referring to it as a masterpiece.

But, during its first centuries in France, it became "just another painting by a master." It was not even considered by most to be Leonardo's best painting. Sometime after Leonardo's death it eventually moved with King Francis I from Amboise to his newly renovated Fontainebleau. The *Mona Lisa* eventually made it to the palace at Versailles where it spent almost two centuries. The Louvre was opened it 1793, and in 1797, the *Mona Lisa* was moved with the other masterpieces from the Versailles to the Louvre. As the Louvre became more accessible to everyday folks, the *Mona Lisa's* popularity slowly began to rise.

In the mid-1800's its standing among masterpieces was slowly increasing. And in the late 1800's, with the help of an

---

[67] His new employer.
[68] The Louvre was opened in 1793, and in 1797 the *Mona Lisa* was sent there with the other paintings from the Versailles. (From 1800 to 1804, it hung in Napoleon's private quarters, instead of the Louvre.)

ever increasing international press, *Mona Lisa's* smile began receiving attention.

And then one day, in the days of less-stringent security in the Louvre, something happened to greatly increase the *Mona Lisa's* popularity. On a Sunday in 1911 an Italian man, Vincenzo Peruggia, was working in the museum. But on this day, instead of leaving after the work day, he hid in a closet. The next day the museum was closed. He came out of the closet, took the *Mona Lisa* off the wall and out of its frame, and left the museum with the painting hidden under his clothes.[69]

The theft was not even discovered until the following day, after the museum had opened again. A local artist had come to the museum, as was his custom, to paint a copy of the *Mona Lisa*.[70] As he was setting up his equipment, he realized that the *Mona Lisa* was not hanging in her spot on the wall. He enquired of a guard as to where the painting had gone. The guard assumed the painting had been removed to the museum photo studio to be photographed. Time passed and the painting did not return. The local painter finally bribed the guard to go check on it. Lo and behold, it was not there. The museum was immediately sealed off as a search for the missing painting began. Alas, it was gone. People leaving Paris and France were searched for the painting as well, but it was not discovered.[71]

---

[69] He could not have rolled the picture, like the thief in *Ever After*. It was painted on poplar wood.

[70] He routinely did this, and sold the copies to visitors.

[71] The painting remained in hiding for two years (possibly in France the entire time).

The robbery made headline news across the world. People mourned for the *Mona Lisa*, songs were written to her, flowers were brought to her empty spot at the museum. And for two years, the clues to her disappearance were almost non-existent: museum security blamed the Paris police for not finding more clues, and of course the police blamed the museum for having bad security. Rumors flew. One was that a rich millionaire from the U.S. had paid to have the painting stolen, and another that the Germans had stolen it to make the French look bad. (World War I was lurking in the not-too distant future.)

Those rumors were all eventually shown to be incorrect. Two years after its disappearance, after most had given up on ever seeing the painting again, an Italian art dealer placed a routine ad that he was looking for good art to buy. He received a mysterious response to his ad – from a "Leonardo" who claimed to have the *Mona Lisa* for sale. Needless to say the art dealer was a bit suspicious – many folks had claimed to have the painting during the previous two years.

The dealer showed up at the apartment of the man who claimed to have the *Mona Lisa*. He brought with him a friend from the local art museum. "Leonardo" unpacked a large crate, removed a false bottom, and then removed the painting. Lo and behold, it was the Mona Lisa (as proven by the Louvre seal on the back of the painting).

Playing it cool, the two art experts informed "Leonardo" that they would have to take the painting with them to compare it to some of Leonardo's other work, to check its authenticity. The thief allowed them to leave the apartment with the painting, at which time they promptly called the police and he

71

was arrested. As a loyal Italian, he claimed he only wanted the painting back in Italy "where it belonged"! (After his trial, he spent less than a year in jail, of the three years the prosecuting lawyer had asked for – and to this day it is unknown whether he actually worked alone, as he claimed he had done.)

After her rediscovery, the Mona Lisa was taken on tour to several major cities in Italy and then returned to her home in France. She stayed there without incident for the next fifty years or so, except during World War II when she was removed from the Louvre along with other important artwork and moved numerous times to avoid destruction or theft.

The next time Mona Lisa came out of the Louvre was in a political move. John F. Kennedy was the U.S. president, and the French were much enamored with the Kennedy family. France decided to grant the United States' request to "borrow" the Mona Lisa for a short time. A special packing crate was made for her and she was shipped to the United States under heavy security. She was exhibited in Washington D.C. for several weeks, and then was taken to New York City for display. Over 1 ½ million Americans viewed the painting at the two locations before she was returned to her spot in France.

In 1974, Mona Lisa traveled by plane to Tokyo and then Moscow, and was seen by two million viewers. It was for this journey that a special bullet proof case was made for the Mona Lisa, and she remains in it, the only painting in the Louvre that is so protected. Then the painting was returned to her home in France, where she remains to this day.

Before her theft, Mona Lisa was already considered a world-class painting. But since her theft and recovery, the painting's fame across the world has increased significantly. The Mona Lisa became the subject of an increasing number of poems, stories, and songs, while "the smile" became a bigger and bigger part of her fame.

Today, most who think of Leonardo da Vinci, think first of his Mona Lisa, and most who think of her, think immediately of her smile.

Travel Years
Leonardo
and Nature Studies

"If you wish to represent a tempest, consider its effects as seen and arrange well, when the wind, blowing over the face of the sea and earth, removes and carries with it such things as are not fixed to the general mass."

From Leonardo's youth, he was fascinated by severe weather – tornados, earthquakes, and the like. He did countless drawings showing the effects of severe storms. Even his architectural studies took weather into consideration – he was intent on planning buildings so that they were strong enough to withstand earthquakes.

As much imagination as Leonardo must have had to do everything he did, his artwork came from real life – oftentimes nature. Leonardo also drew many plants in his notebooks, studying the specimens intently as he drew them. Botany quickly became another side interest. Even when he drew imaginary animals, Leonardo used real animals as his models.

Another story from Leonardo's youth goes like this: While he was still living in Vinci, his father was given the commission for painting a shield. Leonardo painted an imaginary animal on the shield that was very scary.[72] He positioned it in such a way that his father saw the animal without realizing he was looking at a painting – and he was scared! Leonardo had succeeded.[73]

He especially liked horses and birds. He would often buy caged birds, just so that he could set them free. His notebooks show lots of sketches of horses and birds, and occasionally other animals.

In fact, Leonardo liked animals so much that he became a vegetarian, which was very unusual in those days.

---

[72] Though the animal was imaginary, Leonardo had used the features of several different real animals to make it.
[73] His father would go on to sell the shield for much money, and deliver a different shield to the man who had originally commissioned him.

Travel Years Leonardo's Fables and Tales

"Consult nature in everything and write it down."

Like Aesop before him, and Rudyard Kipling after him, Leonardo liked to write short stories, typically with animals as the subjects, and a moral message as a conclusion. His fables and tales were often pointed, and often humorous.

One of his many fables: "A rat was besieged in his little dwelling by a weasel, which with unwearied vigilance awaited his surrender, while watching his imminent peril through a little hole. Meanwhile the cat came by and suddenly seized the weasel and forthwith devoured it. Then the rat offered up a sacrifice to Jove of some of his store of nuts, humbly thanking his providence, and came out of his hole to enjoy his lately lost liberty. But he was instantly deprived of it, together with his life, by the cruel claws and teeth of the lurking cat."[74]

After reading Leonardo's fables, one of my students, David Cox, wrote his own: "There was once a lazy fly who loved macaroni, but he hated making it. So he decided to try to trick someone else into making macaroni for him. He decided to put up a sign on the town bulletin. The sign read, 'Help Wanted'. Later that day, the fly gets a call, 'I'll help.' So at 7:00 the spider came over to help make the mac and cheese and eats the fly and the macaroni and cheese. The moral of this story is: Make your own mac and cheese."

Leonardo also wrote many humorous tales. One of them went like this: "A man was desired to rise from bed, because the sun was already risen. To which he replied: "I had was desired to rise from bed, because the sun was already risen. To which he replied: "If I had as far to go, and as much to do as he has, I should be risen by now; but having but a little way to go, I shall not rise yet."[75]

---

[74] This fable is one of the nineteen fables translated from Italian in *The Notebooks of Leonardo da Vinci, Volume 1.*
[75]The tale is from *The Notebooks of Leonardo da Vinci, Volume 1*, page 352.

Travel Years
Leonardo and Anatomy

"The painter who is familiar with the nature of the sinews, muscles, and tendons, will know very well, in giving movement to a limb, how many and which sinews cause it."

Anatomy is the study of the structure of living things. Leonardo da Vinci was very interested in anatomy because it allowed him to be a better painter. As he studied the human body, plants, and animals, he was able to draw and paint them more accurately.

Leonardo's anatomical studies are among his greatest contributions to science. Here his artistic ability is combined with his observation skills and imagination. In fact, in his time he was considered by some to be the greatest anatomist in the world. He is credited with being the first to make anatomical drawings in the manner still used today – using four sketches to show each part. He was the first to make cross-sectional drawings of the body showing veins, arteries, and nerves in this manner. Thus he was the first to make anatomy studies truly a visual science, relying primarily on an abundance of pictures rather than words. One of Leonardo's most incredible drawings is that of the "Embryo in the Womb." It takes my breath away to see something so "pro-life" that was drawn five hundred years ago!

Leonardo actually knew more about the workings of the human body than most doctors in his day. As a painter, he was particularly interested in the way the eyes worked. To see was to perceive, was to be able to draw... Leonardo also studied the skeletal system. And in the last years of his life he studied the heart. He began his study of the heart with studies of cows' hearts. He compared the flow of blood to the flow of water.

Over the years, Leonardo dissected animals occasionally, including bears, cows, frogs, horses, monkeys, and pigs, though he preferred to do human dissections.

Leonardo drew his "Vitruvian Man"[76] to show the "ideal proportions" of the human body. He based those proportions on his studies of the human body through the years, and the measurements he had taken. It was not an idea that originated with Leonardo – but once again he was the one who took it to a higher level. His notebooks contain countless entries describing the various proportions he had observed and measured.

---

[76] Shown in *Appendix A*.

In 1507, after witnessing the death of an old man at a hospital in Florence, Leonardo's interest was sparked again. The old man died very peaceably, and Leonardo was allowed to do a study of his body in an attempt to determine why the man had died.

Leonardo did a few more human dissections during the first few years of his anatomy studies, moving up to more than ten in 1509 alone.

For a short period of time, probably from 1510 – 1511, Leonardo did dissections with Della Torra, an anatomy professor, and the leading anatomist of their age, at the University in Pavia, near Milan. By time he died, da Vinci had done more than thirty human dissections and had completed thousands of anatomical drawings.

Leonardo had kept his anatomical studies mostly a secret during his life time. In 1510 he made plans to publish his anatomy studies of the entire human body, plans that were never carried out.

Final Years – Overview

Leonardo da Vinci was in Rome from 1514 to 1516. Leonardo had hoped to join Michelangelo and Raphael doing great artwork for the Pope, the head of the Roman Catholic Church, but his reputation of not completing projects had preceded him, and the Pope wasn't interested in hiring him. Leonardo did more of his scientific work in those years in Rome.

He also traveled to Pavia, Bologna, and Milan during that time.

In 1515, Leonardo was accused of sorcery, because of his work dissecting dead bodies. At that point, the Pope, as the "law of the land," banned Leonardo from performing any further human dissections.

During that time there were several other artists in Rome doing work for the Pope, and Donato Bramante was building St. Peters Cathedral. But, apparently Leonardo had little contact with the other artists at this time, and may have been quite lonely at this period of his life. This may have contributed to his acceptance when the King of France offered him a new job, in France.

Leonardo built a mechanical lion in 1515 for the celebrations in conjunction with the coronation of Francis I, King of France. The lion was capable of movement; and when it opened its mouth, it revealed lilies. Leonardo's lion was written about in other contemporary accounts, not just his own.

In 1515, the new French King, Francis I, traveled into northern Italy to prove his strength against those in that area.

Francis I was the French king who had formed a large royal library and appointed a royal librarian. He had a deep interest in the arts and sciences. While in Italy, he met Leonardo da Vinci and invited him to France.

Final Years
Leonardo in Rome

Of his mint at Rome, Leonardo said, *"It can also be made without a spring. But the screw above must always be joined to the part of the movable sheath...all the coins should be a perfect circle."*

Leonardo da Vinci moved to Rome under the patronage of Giuliano de Medici, Pope Leo X's brother.

Leonardo opened an art studio in Rome, but he was given no major assignments, in spite of receiving a generous monthly stipend from Giuliano. Instead of doing great art in Rome, Leonardo worked on his scientific studies and designed a machine for the Pope to mint coins. Banking and coin minting had almost disappeared completely in Europe during the Middle Ages; at the time of the Renaissance, both were slowly coming back. Surprisingly, the invention of the printing press led first to advancements in minting coins, rather than printing bills. Leonardo used the same principles from the printing press (which had borrowed ideas from grape presses) to develop his machine to mill coins – a method that led to greater uniformity in size and weight.[77]

---

[77] Milled coins also made it more difficult to "shave" the edges of coins.

Final Years
Leonardo in France

King Francis I's comment about Leonardo da Vinci: "... did not believe that there had ever been another man born into the world who had known so much as Leonardo, and this not only in matters concerning Sculpture, Painting and Architecture, but because he was a great Philosopher."

Leonardo accepted the French King's invitation, and in 1516, he left Italy for good, going to France to be the *Premier Painter and Engineer and Architect of the King.* He lived in a chateau, in Amboise, near the king's palace, receiving a generous annual stipend from his new patron. He was treated almost like a guest, and Leonardo's primary job was to have intellectual discussions with the king! Occasional scientific and architectural studies filled some of his time there as well.

Even though he suffered from a stroke during this time, these last years of his life were the easiest for him. At Leonardo's death, he apologized to "God and Man for leaving so much undone." He died at Amboise in 1519.

Stories vary as to whether Francis I was present when Leonardo died. His earliest biography had the king at Leonardo's side when Leonardo died. Later sources said this was impossible since the king was in another part of France at the time.[78]

_____

[78] And even later, sources said the king was not elsewhere and <u>could</u> have been with Leonardo!

"Thou, O God, dost sell us all good things at the price of labor."

Conclusion

Leonardo da Vinci was a fascinating man, who did fascinating work in a wide variety of areas. For a time, his reputation was of being someone who didn't complete what he started, and that certainly was one of his problems. But in the end, he accomplished much. And what he did accomplish set the stage for many that came after him.

He was the earliest of the "High Renaissance" artists – and one of the better known. Through him, we can gain a better understanding of the times he lived in, as well as of him and his work.

Leonardo is often thought of as a great artist. And he certainly was that. But he was so much more – a dreamer who looked so far beyond the obvious – an architect, a mathematician, a scientist, a musician, and more!

I hope this brief introduction to Leonardo da Vinci, enabled you to learn more about him and his incredible work.

Appendix A
Leonardo's
"Vitruvian Man"

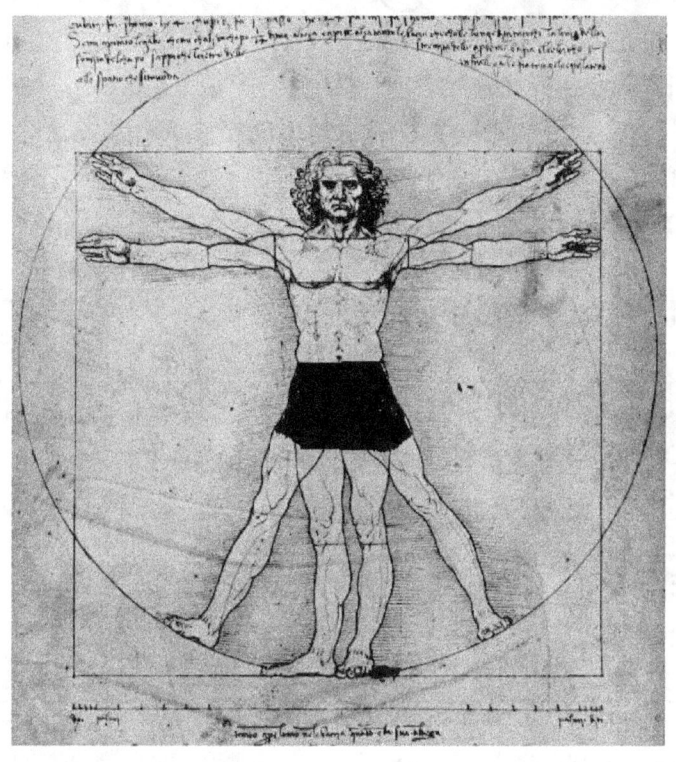

Leonardo da Vinci drew his "Vitruvian Man" to demonstrate the ideal proportions of the human body. Leonardo was not the first to come up with this idea – Vitruvius, a Roman architect and engineer 1400 years before Leonardo, had come up with similar measurements – Leonardo took it to the next "logical" step, and drew the man he was describing. The charts on the next two pages show some of the proportions Leonardo had derived.

Appendix B
Human Proportions
According to da Vinci

While the similarities Leonardo "discovered" don't hold true on each individual person, they are close in a surprising number of cases.

Between shoulder bones	Between hip bones	
Mouth to bottom of Chin	Big toe	1/6 of foot
From wrist to elbow, and elbow to armpit (when arm is bent).		Length of one foot
From the fissure (opening) of the mouth, to the bottom of nose		1/7 of the face
The mouth to the bottom of the chin	The mouth's length	1/4 of the face
The end of the eye socket (towards the ear), to your ear	The length of the ear	1/3 of the face
The middle of the nose to the bottom of chin		1/2 of the face
The eyebrows to the bottom of the chin		2/3 of the face

Beginning of hair to the bottom of the chin	The hand	1/10 of height
One hand	1/3 of the arm	1/9 of height
Full head		1/8 of height
The foot	Face	1/7 of height
Top of the chest to the crown (top) of the head		1/6 of height
From elbow to the wrist		1/5 of height
The max width of the shoulders	The sole of foot to lower edge of knee	1/4 of height
Arms out full length		Full height

Actual Measurements Compared to Predictions

Measurements in inches or centimeters	Name	Name	Name	Name
Height				
= Arm span				
Kneeling				
= 3/4 Height				
Elbow to Wrist				
= 1/5 Height				
Foot				
= Face				
= 1/7 Height				
Middle of nose to bottom of chin				
= 1/2 Face				
Mouth to bottom of chin				
= 1/4 Face				

Explanation: Measure body section, listed in each section of chart. Calculate each of the fractions shown (3/4 Height, 1/2 Face, etc.) Compare – do the measurements in each section = the calculated ones Leonardo predicted? (Typically, some do, and some don't.) *You may want to copy the chart and fill it out with your family or class.*

Appendix C
Leonardo's Early Years
(Anchiano, Vinci, and Florence)

Dates	Events in Leonardo's Life	Related Events	World Events
1452	Leonardo's Birth at <u>Anchiano</u>, two miles from <u>Vinci</u>.		
1453		Constantinople falls to the Ottoman Turks, bringing an end to the Byzantine Empire.	*100 Years' War* between France and England finally ends.
c.1455	Leonardo moves to <u>Vinci</u> to live with Grandparents		First Gutenberg Bible printed.
c.1466	Moves to <u>Florence</u> with his father to apprentice in Andrea Verrocchio's workshop.		Birth of Desiderius Erasmus.

Dates	Events in Leonardo's Life	Related Events	World Events
1469		Birth of Nicolo Machiavelli in Florence; Giuliano de Medici becomes new ruler of Florence.	
1472	Leonardo paints angel in Verrocchio's *Baptism of Christ* (left hand corner); also accepted into Painters' Guild that year.		Dante's *Divine Comedy* printed.
1473	Landscape Drawing, his oldest surviving drawing.		Birth of Nicolaus Copernicus.
1475		Birth of Michelangelo	

Dates	Events in Leonardo's Life	Related Events	World Events
1476	Leonardo's first younger sibling is born.	Birth of Cesare Borgia (his father will later become Pope Alexander VI). Galeazzo Sforza is assassinated in Milan.	
1477	Starts own workshop; Commissioned for altar-piece for chapel. (Contract almost passed to someone else in 1483!)	Lorenzo de Medici[79] takes power in Florence, after his brother Guiliano's death.	
1480	Leonardo works for Lorenzo de Medici[80].	Ludovico Sforza takes power in Milan.	Birth of Ferdinand Magellan.

---

[79] "Lorenzo the Magnificent"
[80] Lorenzo was a patron of the arts, like his father and grandfather before him.

Dates	Events in Leonardo's Life	Related Events	World Events
1481	Commissioned for *Adoration of the Magi*, 1st large painting – which like so many others, he leaves unfinished!	Florentine painters go to Rome to decorate Sistine Chapel.	
1482	Leonardo offers service as engineer, architect, sculptor... to Duke of Milan, in famous letter.	Euclid's book *Elements* printed in Latin for first time.	

Milan Years

Dates	Leonardo's Life	Related Events	World Events
1483	Moves to <u>Milan</u>; contracted for first *Virgin of the Rocks*, doesn't finish; starts equestrian statue for Duke of Milan.[81]	Birth of Raphael.	Martin Luther is born in Germany.
1484 & 1485		Plagues in Milan.	
1488	First Anatomical drawings appear in his notebooks.	Duke considers finding another sculptor for his equestrian statue. Verrocchio dies.	

---

[81] i.e., he begins initial sketches!

Dates	Leonardo's Life	Related Events	World Events
1490	Leonardo directs feasts and pageants; starts serious work in notebooks; sketches plan for *Treatise on Painting*; makes scale model for statue; considers making a telescope.		
1492		Lorenzo de Medici dies; all of Florence attends funeral.	Christopher Columbus discovers America.
1493	Builds full-scale clay model of equestrian statue, unveiled for wedding.	Maximilian I becomes Holy Roman Emperor, and marries Bianca Sforza, daughter of Duke of Milan.	

Dates	Leonardo's Life	Related Events	World:
1494	Paints second *Virgin of the Rocks;* begins construction of canal and molds for statue. He also spends some time in <u>Pavia</u> studying.	Sforza family "invites" French King Charles VIII, who invades Italy; Medici family falls from power in Florence. Machiavelli enters public office in Florence. Luca Pacioli writes book on accounting methods.	
1495	Begins *Last Supper* in dining room at the Santa Maria delle Grazie (finishes in 1497). Also teaches himself Latin and sketches a robot.	Donato Bramante works on dome for Santa Maria delle Grazie.	
1496		Luca Pacioli comes to Milan to teach mathematics.	Copernicus studies in Italy.
1497	Pacioli works on geometry book, *On Divine Proportion*. Leonardo illustrates it.		

Dates	Leonardo's Life	Related Events	World Events
1498	Leonardo plans to publish his notebooks; writes book on theory of mechanics. He meets with other artists to discuss artistic theories.	Louis XII becomes King of France. (Pope annuls Louis' marriage, and arranges for Pope's son, Cesare Borgia, to marry French princess.)	
1499	Leonardo's clay horse is destroyed by French soldiers invading Milan.	Duke Ludovico is driven out of Milan by French troops. Borgia begins subduing Italian cities, with the French King, Louis XII.	Ottoman Empire wages war against Venice (1499 – 1501).

Travel Years

Dates	Leonardo's Life	Related Events	World Events
1500	Leonardo leaves Milan after it falls to French; he stays briefly in Vaprio and Mantua; makes short visit to Venice before returning to Florence. Begins 10-year work on *Madonna and Child with St Anne*. *Last Supper* is already deteriorating.	Cesare Borgia enters Rome as the conqueror of Romagna. (Caterina Sforza is one of the conquered leaders.) Machiavelli visits French king, Louis XII, to enlist aid for Florence's fight against Pisa.	
1501	Sketch for *Madonna and Child with St. Anne* exhibited.	Borgia made Duke of Romagna by the Pope.	Michelangelo is in Rome.

Dates	Leonardo's Life	Related Events	World Events
1502	Leonardo serves as military engineer and cartographer to Cesare Borgia; traveling with the army throughout Romagna. / Designs bridge for the Sultan.	Machiavelli serves as envoy to Cesare Borgia. Cesare subdues more central Italian cities.	France and Spain are at war with each other.
1503	Returns to Florence to great honors. Commissioned for painting of *Battle of Anghiari*; begins *Mona Lisa* (working off and on on both). He also works on plans for canal from Florence to the sea and experiments with flying.	Machiavelli is in Rome for the election of the new Pope, Julius II, after death of Pope Alexander VI. Borgia is poisoned. French defeated in Italy. Machiavelli returns to Florence.	

Dates	Leonardo's Life	Related Events	World Events
1504	Leonardo's father dies, leaving behind twelve children, and no will. [82] Leonardo receives nothing from the estate.	Raphael moves to Florence, studies with Leonardo (and later Michelangelo).	Michelangelo finishes *David* sculpture.
1505	Finishes full-size sketch of *Battle* painting; does many nature sketches.	Michelangelo starts *Battle of Cascina* on wall across from Leonardo; but is called to Rome before he finishes his painting.	
1506	Summoned to <u>Milan</u> by the French governor of the city; stops work on *Battle* painting;[83] finishes *Mona Lisa*.		

---

[82] A member of the legal profession, who should have known better.
[83] The summons was not the reason he stopped the battle painting, problems with the painting were.

Dates	Leonardo's Life	Related Events	World Events
1507	Brief trip back to Florence; makes plans again to publish notebooks. Uncle dies, leaving everything to Leonardo.		
1508	Returns to Milan, where he is employed by French King Louis XII, currently living there. Asked to make statue for victor in Milan, Trivulzio. Begins major anatomical research.	Pope Julius II and Emperor Maximilian I form an alliance.	Michelangelo begins work on ceiling of Sistine Chapel. (Finishes in 1512)

Final Years

Dates	Leonardo's Life	Related Events	World Events
1509			Henry VIII becomes King of England.
1510			Martin Luther visits Rome.
1512		Medici family back in power in Florence, after Swiss defeat French in Italy with help of Pope Julius II's Holy Roman League.	
1513	Leonardo goes to Rome, at request of Pope Leo X's brother, Giuliano. He opens art studio but concentrates on his science work.	French leave Italy; Machiavelli is imprisoned, released, and then writes *The Prince*. Leo X becomes next Pope.	Raphael and Michelangelo are busy painting in Rome.

Dates	Leonardo's Life	Related Events	World Events
1514	Back in Florence for a short time, paints only self-portrait.[84]	Francis I becomes King of France.	
1515	Travels to Pavia, Bologna, and Milan. Constructs mechanical lion for Francis I's coronation; is forbidden by Pope from doing more human dissections. Paints last known picture: *St John the Baptist*.	Guiliano de Medici leaves Rome, dies soon afterwards.	
1516	Leonardo moves to Amboise, France to work for King Francis I as "Premier Painter and Engineer and Architect of the King." His right hand is paralyzed by a stroke.		Charles V becomes king of Spain. Sir Thomas More publishes *Utopia*.

---

[84] Shown on the Front Cover. (Some historians list the date as 1512.) Some art historians even debate whether it was actually a self-portrait.

Dates	Leonardo's Life	Related Events	World Events
1517			Martin Luther's *95 Theses* on the Church door.[85]
1519	Leonardo writes his will on April 23rd, dies on May 2nd.		Ferdinand Magellan begins expedition around the world. Hernando Cortez lands in Mexico.

---

[85] Reformation begins with this event.

After Leonardo's Life

Dates	Related Events
1550	Giorgio Vasari writes his first edition of *Lives of the Artists*, which includes the first biography of Leonardo da Vinci.
1570	Melzi dies, before finishing work on Leonardo's *Treatise on Painting*. Dispersion of the pages of Leonardo's notebooks begins.
1651	Leonardo's *Treatise on Painting* is published.
1652	A door is cut in the wall of the *Last Supper.*
1796	French soldiers deface *Last Supper*.
1797	*Mona Lisa* moved to the Louvre, from Versailles.
1800	*Mona Lisa* hangs in Napoleon's bedroom.
1836 & 1845	Bridges finally built where Leonardo had planned one, across mouth of Black Sea.
1911	*Mona Lisa* is stolen.
1913	*Mona Lisa* recovered.
1963	*Mona Lisa* visits U.S.
1974	*Mona Lisa* is encased in a special bullet proof glass box before she visits Tokyo and Moscow, and then returns to France "for good."
1977	Major restoration begins on *The Last Supper*. Idea for *Leonardo's Horse* comes to Charles Dent, in the U.S.
1990's	A "Da Vinci" Robot is built.
1999	Restoration of *The Last Supper* is completed. *Leonardo's Horse* is unveiled in Milan. A working parachute, based on Leonardo's plans, is built and tried out.
2002	*Leonardo's Bridge* is built in Norway.

Appendix D
Leonardo's
Contemporaries
(1452 – 1519)

- Johannes Gutenberg (1398-1468) – inventor of the Western printing press
- Pope Alexander VI, born "Rodrigo Borgia" (1431 – 1503)
- Andrea Verrocchio (1435 – 1488) – Italian artist, musician, goldsmith
- Pope Julius II, born "Giulano della Rovere" (1443 – 1513)
- Donato Bramante (1444 – 1514) – Italian architect
- Luca Pacioli (1445 – 1514) – Italian mathematician
- Christopher Columbus (1451 – 1506) – Italian/Spanish explorer
- King Henry VII (1457 – 1509) – King of England
- Maximilian I (1459 – 1519) – Holy Roman Emperor
- King Louis XII (1462 – 1515) – King of France, cousin of King Charles VII
- Desiderius Erasmus (1466-1536) – Dutch reformer
- Niccolo Machiavelli (1469 –1527) – Italian political thinker, author of The Prince
- King Charles VIII (1470 – 1498) – King of France
- Albrecht Durer (1471-1528) – German painter, scholar, and author
- Nicolaus Copernicus (1473-1543) – Polish astronomer

- (Buonarroti) Michelangelo (1475-1564) – Italian artist
- Pope Leo X, born "Giovanni de Medici" (1475 – 1521)
- Cesare Borgia (1475 – 1507) – notorious Italian military dictator
- Sir Thomas More (1478-1535) English statesman, wrote *Utopia,* wouldn't recognize King Henry VIII as head of church in England (movie about them: *Man for All Seasons*)
- Ferdinand Magellan (1480 – 1521) – Portuguese explorer
- Raphael, born "Raffaello Sanzio" (1483-1520) – another great Italian artist
- Martin Luther (1483-1546) "Father" of the Protestant Reformation
- Hernando Cortez (1485 – 1547) Spanish explorer of the New World
- Titian, born "Tiziano Vecellio" (1477-1576) – Italian artist
- King Henry VIII, King of England (1491 – 1547)
- King Francis I, King of France (1494 – 1547)
- Charles, grandson of Ferdinand and Isabella (1500 – 1558) – ruled as Charles I of Spain, beginning in 1516, and Charles V, Holy Roman Emperor, beginning in 1519.
- Giorgio Vasari (1511 – 1574) Italian artist and author of *Lives of the Artists*

Other noteworthy folks who lived soon after him included:
- Tycho Brahe (1546-1601) – Danish astronomer
- William Shakespeare (1564-1616) – English author
- Galileo (1564-1642) – Italian scientist

Appendix E
Bibliography:
Books & Web Pages

Leonardo da Vinci, General:

Bacci, Mina *Leonardo* Copyright 1978, Fabbri Editori Milan, Italy.

Herbert, Janis *Leonardo da Vinci for Kids* Copyright 1998, Chicago Review Press, Inc. Chicago Illinois.

Langley, Andrew *Leonardo and His Times* Copyright 1999, Dorling Kindersley, Inc., New York New York.

Reti, Ladislao *The Unknown Leonardo* Copyright 1974, McGraw-Hill Book Co. Maidenhead England.

Richter, Jean Paul *The Notebooks of Leonardo Da Vinci Volumes I and II* Copyright 1970, Dover Publications, Inc. New York.

Ripley, Elizabeth *Leonardo Da Vinci* Copyright 1952, Oxford University Press, Inc. United States.

Vallentin, Antonina *Leonardo Da Vinci* Copyright 1938, The Viking Press, Inc., New York.

Zollner, Frank *Leonardo* Copyright 2001, Taschen Gmbh Germany.

Zubov, V.P., translated by David H. Kraus *Leonardo da Vinci*, Copyright 1968, Barnes & Noble Inc, New York.

http://www.mos.org/leonardo/
http://www.lairweb.org.nz/leonardo/index.html#stages
www.museoscienza.org/english/leonardo

Anatomy:
http://mathforum.org/alejandre/frisbie/math/leonardo.html

Art:
Da Vinci, Leonardo, edited by Andre Chatel, translated by
ellen Callmann. *Leonardo on Art and the Artist* Copyright
1961, Published in 2002 by Dover Publications, New
York.

Bridge:
http://news.bbc.co.uk/2/hi/europe/1630792.stm

Drawings/Sketches:
Da Vinci, Leonardo *Leonardo Drawings, 60 Works by*
Leonardo da Vinci Copyright 1980 Dover
Publications, Inc.

http://europe.cnn.com/2001/WORLD/europe/07/10/uk.vinci/

Horse:
Fritz, Jean *Leonardo's Horse* Copyright 2001, G.P. Putnam's
Son, Fogelsville, Pennsylvania.

Inventions:
Cooper, Margaret *The Inventions of Leonardo da Vinci*
Copyright 1965, Macmillan Company, New York.

Last Supper:
http://arthistory.about.com/gi/dynamic/offsite.htm?site=htt
p://www.ebtx.com/art/art28.htm

Mona Lisa:
Sasson, Donald *Becoming Mona Lisa* Copyright 2001,
    Harcourt Inc. Orlando, Florida.

http://www.pbs.org/treasuresoftheworld/mona_lisa/mlevel_1/mtimeline.html

Paintings:
http://www.ibiblio.org/wm/paint/auth/vinci/
http://www.theartgallery.com.au/ArtEducation/greatartists/DaVinci/

www.ingramcontent.com/pod-product-compliance
Lightning Source LLC
Chambersburg PA
CBHW081135170526
45165CB00008B/2683